Because

I

Can

Hanieh Khoshkhou

PUBLISHED BY PEACOCK PRESS

PEACOCK PRESS

Peacock Press Inc.

Ottawa, ON

Peacock Press Canada edition October 2019

Copyright© 2019 Hanieh Khoshkhou

Edited by Shabana Ansari

Cover design by Sanchita Jain

Interior design by Nicole Cuillerier

Library and Archives Canada Cataloguing in
Publication

Khoshkhou, Hanieh, author

Because I Can/Hanieh Khoshkhou

Issued in print and electronic formats

ISBN 978-1-9992144-0-1 (paperback)

ISBN 978-1-9992144-1-8 (ebook)

For you maman,

Because you have been my
everything.

Unfulfilled destinies

Your death has left a
permanent hole in my heart.

I daydream about you still being
here.

I have tried to find other men
like you. I have not succeeded.

I still haven't called your mom
to let her know I too share her
grief.

Your death was like an atomic
bomb that wiped away anything
that mattered.

I tried so hard to get you on the
right path. Nothing worked.

I don't hear your voice
anymore when you come to me
in my dreams.

Do you hear me when I scold
you from down here?!

No one has come close to
making me feel the way you
did.

Why hasn't our destiny fallen
into place yet? Why can't we get
it right?

I miss you. All. The time.

I can't believe how easily my
tears drop when I think about
you.

If only I could hear you say
"bébé, je t'aime" again.

I think about how life would be
different if you had just *listened*
more and *reacted* less.

Even your mom agreed with me.

You have been the only one the family still likes.

Maman

Your unconditional love and
support have been everything
to us.

You have saved me so many
times I don't know what I
would do without you.

I'm less alone when I talk to
you.

I pray to reincarnate as your
daughter every time. You're so
good at it.

I don't like it when others refer
to you as "mom". ¿Don't they
know you belong only to me?

I wish I was more like you.

Your love fills everyone that
has come in contact with you.

That's why no one can say no
to you.

You are everything.

My only goal in life has been to
make you proud of me.
Nothing else has mattered.

"I don't ever want you to look
with desperation at a man when
he reaches his hand for his
wallet. Always make your own
money."

I'm sorry I worry you. I try not
to. But you still get it out of me.

When I hug you, and lie beside
you, I feel like I'm home.

You have been my greatest
blessing.

I wish you didn't smoke so much.

Your voice calms and reassures me. I wouldn't be who I am if it wasn't for you.

You are a warrior when it comes to protecting your children.

You raised us differently. And you know that.

You deserve the Nobel for having stayed with him.

You didn't have to sacrifice yourself for us. We would have been ok.

Pedar

funfar: cradling the top of your foot while I sit, and you swing me from side to side. This was the best part of my childhood.

Men like you

My heart longs for you.

Every part of my body feels like
it's floating when you look into
my eyes.

I love the wrinkles around and
above your eyebrows when you
ask me a question.

Your hearty laugh affirms your
affections for me.

You took my breath away when
you leaned in and picked off
the one eye lash off my face.

I long for the day that you tell
me you want to be with me.

You want me to be vulnerable
with you, but yet you reject me.

Why do you punish us like this?
Why do you deny us this feeling
that I know could last forever
and ever? Are you actually blind
to it all, or am I not good
enough for you?

I see stars in your eyes when
you look at me.

The dense bullshit you say
makes me wonder why I pick
men like you.

When you tell me to do shit, I
can't believe a man actually had
the courage to TELL ME to do
something! In that moment, I
want you all wrapped up inside
of me.

I don't know if I'm making all this shit up in my head, or actually living it. You have that effect on me.

When you hold my hand and I see your fingers folding in without any hesitation.

The little song you made me.

When you call me by my last name.

Our back and forth banter.

When you tell me that I'm amazing and then turn around and tell me that you don't want to be with me. What the FUCK is that?! Why am I not good enough?

You don't get upset with any of the racist shit I throw at you about: you, your accent or your ethnicity. I love that you know I'm joking with you. I love that you will do "Canadian" accent right on the spot when I ask you to.

Even though you try to be "indifferent" in front of your friends, you totally come across as someone who is interested in me. Your dumb ass doesn't even realize you're doing this!

I want to stand beside you. And you lean into me while holding me across my shoulder to order our Timmies together.

I can't believe how silent you
are when you sleep. It's a
complete contrast to everything
about you. Even you need a
break from YOU when you
sleep.

When we talk about different
business ideas, I constantly
come up with a better version
of what you are suggesting in
my head. You are just too quick
to shoot down the ideas.

When you refused to give me
the cigarette.

There's a part of me that wants
to completely avoid talking to
you about all my thoughts
when it comes to religion or
homosexuality. I know we
already clash on these topics.
How can I still want to be with

someone who has these opposing views? These are moments when I question my own sanity.

You don't get to use my knowledge and strength in business, and then turn around and tell me you want to be with another woman! This is why I stepped away from you. Don't you know, you can't have your cake and eat it too!?

I would want to have a kid with you. Even though it goes against everything I have always said about becoming a parent. I know you would be there with me. Throughout it all.

Every time I have to spell out
my full name, I can hear you
rolling your eyes.

It's been 3 months, how are
you still pronouncing my name
wrong?

Yes, my hair is just like that. All
the time. Don't touch it.

No, I'm not afraid of success!
That's what people who have
been privileged all their lives
fear.

When will I finally be a
Canadian?

"Toronto. Toronto. Do you
want to know where I was
born?"

— *When you're a person of colour*

I hate Heather too.

When you wouldn't get invited to the sleepovers because you were the only one that was an immigrant.

"Why don't you just go back to your country?" I can't. There's no going back.

When your childhood memories are of the war, wall shaking underground tunnels and bombs dropping.

The teacher didn't get him to go to the front of the class to slap him with the wooden ruler on his palms. Where am I??!!

I don't have to sit in the back because I'm the tallest and biggest?

Mrs. Hallam. Saved me. Taught me everything.

I don't understand the swirly handwriting on the board.

If you *sound* like them. They will be your *friends*.

— *Newcomer's Childhood*

I do the same work. Better
results. But you still pay him
more.

I pull my hair in and don't wear
bright colours at my interview
because I don't want you to
only see me as my *ethnic* self.

I worry that my strength and
focus scare my male
counterparts all the time.

I feel like I have to squeeze into
shapewear so that everything
gets "smoothed" out. Just to
please your eyes!

How do you walk around
naked so easily and without any
thought to your body?

We run households, manage all
relationships, work full time,
and you still want me to look

rested, beautiful and be pleasant
at the end of the day?

No, I don't want children. No,
I won't change my mind.

If men got periods, there would
be mandatory weekly time off
for them.

I bend in every direction, yet I
am still not *good enough*.

You tell me that if I'm not a
particular size, shape or colour,
I will never be *good enough*.

Why does what I wear and
how I look even matter to my
job performance?

You have no idea to the depths
of my emotions. you. really.
don't.

I don't know why I am
consistently surprised about
your level of ignorance.

You act like teenage boys when
there's a beautiful woman
around. No matter your age.

— *Waving my fist at the man!*

Baradar

If it wasn't for you, I wouldn't
have ever been able to pursue
my adventures the way I did.

You always took care of
everything at home. I will
forever be indebted to you.

Blessed

When I can breathe in without
the worry and anxiety of the
uncertain future filling my
lungs.

It looks like I really have *made
it*.

When you know you are able to
face anything because you
know you can handle it.

"I am not like the others. I am
not average or weak. I am my
mother's daughter. Powerful
and resilient."

"It's OK, Honey. You're
strong. You will get through
this," says my brother to me
trying to console me going
through my *talaq*.

I tell myself to *focus* on my
ability to overcome anything
[this helps (sometimes) with the
anxiety that bubbles in my
throat].

"Intriguing and electrifying" –
this is how the male human
describes me with lust in his
eyes and a bulge in his pants.

"Why don't you lower your
standards?" Because I refuse to
settle the way you did. Argh.

España

"Quítate lo". That was the first
reflexive verb I learnt.

When you're 20 years old and
don't realize all the dangerous
things you did until you
become 40.

Having the rug swept away
right from underneath your feet
for the first time when you get
betrayed.

Aja. You saved me. You let me
talk about *it* for the first time.

Making friends with the drug
dealers and getting a kick out of
them asking us if we want some
cocaine!

That moment when you no
longer see your surroundings
through the eyes of a tourist.

"You really should pay
attention to where you are
leaving your purse. There are
people watching you."

"Venga. Hasta luego.": Every
two steps in Pamplona.

This was the only time that I
drank so much I felt like I was
floating!

If it wasn't for Spain, I
wouldn't have had the courage
to embark in any of the other
adventures that came after.

"Seriously though, who let's
their kid go halfway across the
world without knowing the
language of the country they are
moving to?" I ask my parents
while they roll their eyes at me.

High school

Kookoo sabzi. Ask an Iranian kid
about the horrors of having
their mom packed this for their
lunch.

"Why are you friends with her?
Just come sit with us" — I'm
not you. I won't turn my back
on a friend.

Flag football. Saved me from
the dark place.

Meeting under the stairwells.
No one even knew.

I.H.M.L: I. Hate. My. Life. —
written across every day in my
agenda.

"Just take a drag. You will like
it."—knowing myself well
enough to resist.

I wish I hadn't given up with
the sciences.

Grade 10 French teacher: je
suis présentement bilingue. No
thanks to you of course!

To the guy with the mole on
your upper lip: I had such a
crush on you.

When your brother was the star
football player and no guy
dared come talk to you.

The war

The explosion of the bombs
makes the walls of the
underground tunnel shake.

The worst part: hearing my
fellow classmates scream from
the potential fate lurking for us
just outside.

The red alarm echoes through
the city: it's. happening. again.

In this country, when I look
outside my class window, I
don't see a soldier shooting into
the sky with an artillery
machine gun. How strange!

Endless dust. Everywhere—we
spent more time underground
in the tunnels than we did in
class.

Present time: lightning sounds like bombs dropping. I have to remind myself that we are no longer in war and therefore not in danger. My heart rate takes longer to process this.

Learning English

"But why do we have to stay
here? I miss grandma."

Repeat after the people on the
screen to sound like them.

I don't find a lot of what they
say or do on the TV funny.
Why is there "laughter" in the
background?

Huma: My first. Real. Friend.

No. My name is Hanieh. I
won't change it.

3161 Kingston Rd.

When my mom would make
"pizza" with ketchup on
toasted pita bread. If lucky,
there were cut up hot dogs on it
too.

Thinking by slamming our feet
into the elevator door, it would
finally *arrive*.

Couldn't believe we got that
used couch. Sitting on the
ground all the time has its
limits.

Endless mice. All. The. Time.

"No. We have food at home."
– my brother and I exchange
looks when we were denied
going to the proper pizza store
downstairs to the building!
(*again*)

Sonic the Hedgehog. My
brother over the moon with
father's first real pay.

My fat-self

"You have such a beautiful
face. If you only lose a little
weight you would be *perfect*."

"Are you a vegetarian because
you want to lose weight?"

"Really? You're a vegetarian?
Hmmm."

"You're pretty. And smart. I
just don't date bigger women.
Do you think you can lose
weight?"

"Your stomach. It's bigger than
mine." (on a *date*)

"What do you eat? Tell me."
(unsolicited advice
#1000215245871874887814852
247898)

"It's so slimming. You should buy it."

"Have you ever tried (*insert diet and exercise plan here*)?"

Shrinking myself

Never realized how much I
accommodated other people's
space in relation to my body —
as long as *they* were
comfortable, I would simply
bear whatever discomfort.

I try to please and make *them*
happy. It's OK. It's *easier* for *us*
this *way*.

I wear red lipstick. But I don't
wear dresses/skirts to work.
That's too much attention.

Parsi

When your little hands still
offer me a piece of your eaten
food. You are the epitome of
Maman Farah.

"So, you're a teacher?"—first
time he asked me about what I
do.

The way you come and sit on
my lap as though I'm your
personal human cushion.

You have consistently been one
of my happy thoughts.

When I look into your kind
happy face—I see my brother. I
now understand Khaleh
Faroukh's eyes.

"Who do I love the most in the
WHOLE WIDE world?" – he
responds "MEEE!" with
absolute glee in his voice.

Men

I just don't care enough to
follow up with you.

"No. I'm not going to blow up
your phone or text you all the
time."

Seriously? Just a "hey" as a
response? – delete. App.

When you experience what
ghosting is. After 3 months of
seeing each other.
EVERY.DAY.

Clearly these men were raised
by wolves – 'cause what else
would explain this behaviour?

A.D.H.D.

No. No. Don't fly away with
your other thoughts. You need
to listen to what he's saying.
FOCUS!

Why do I have to sit here with
all these adults? – me asking me
in *another* department meeting.

Fold your hands together. Sit
up and don't float away. You
need this job. Focus on the
questions they are asking you.

I've already answered the
question and analyzed my
response before the interviewer
has even finished asking in my
head—this is how my brain
constantly works.

When I'm really tired and
haven't used my CPAP
machine I struggle with the
focus.

"Make sure Hanieh isn't facing
the TV or any flashing lights.
She will not be present if you
do" – my friends picking on my
little *mental feature*.

*Everything that I have to do that you
don't*

I double check my apartment
locks before going to bed. OK
maybe triple check.

I'm going to slightly move over
to this part of the sidewalk so
this guy can pass me. I don't
like how close he's getting.

Mental note: have your keys in
your hand when walking to
your car in the parking lot. And
walking home. And coming out
of the grocery store. And…

"Do you want to go catch the
sun this weekend?"

— *when it's been so cold for so long*

Ivory Coast

You were so. so. good. It
deserved the whole page to tell
it.

My magic

When your mere concentration
face makes people nervous.

His body language tells me I'm
making him uncomfortable.
How's that possible? I just told
him what I thought—that's *all*.

He pointed me out from deep
in the lineup. "And her". He
tells the bouncer while pointing
at me down the queue. The
people ahead of us part like the
sea—I had just given him a
look.

"Are you angry? Everything
ok?" – yeah, everything is fine.
This is just my face.

Staying away

I've stayed away from it. All.
Of. It. Because I know I
wouldn't give it up if I get
hooked to *it*.

The numbness. The floating.
The escape from it *all*. This is
why I stay away.

My brother echoes the same
fear. This is why he's NEVER
touched *it*.

"No. I've had **one** tonight. No
more. Thanks."

The male "POV"

Has everything else been fixed?
Still have crime? War? And
famine? How about climate
issues? Then why should I give
a shit about contouring non-
fucking-existing lines on my
face?

"Will you grow your nails?"

"You don't dress like a *woman*."

"So, you're saying you don't
need me?"

"Why can't you wear heels?"—
because I weigh 200LBS! And I
fucking like having feeling in
my toes!!

Don't mistake my smiling and
jokes as a sign of weakness—I
can blow you out of the water
with uncanny ease.

"Mom, I'm not going to work
tomorrow."
"Who did you tell off?"

"This is me *relaxed*"—my
response to my Manager who
tells me I have to relax.

– the *other* side

Bullshit fucking jobs

"After 3 years you will be able to order stationery as part of your new tasks." – Lasted 3 weeks before quitting (government position my mom won't let me forget about up until now).

"This time say it with a smile on your face. Trust me it makes such a difference." – one week.

So, I just forward emails. Open fucking mail. Take phone calls and messages. Glad I got that Masters and 4 languages under my belt! – 4 days.

The fluorescent lights. Hated them. Another thing my mom won't let me forget about my workplace complaints.

Solider

After having all that remained
in my stomach thrown up, I
promptly go back to my cubicle
and continue to work. If it
wasn't for my colleague telling
me to go home, I would have
been there till 5pm! – this is
how I *operate*.

"Aren't you tired?" No. I keep
pushing and pushing until the
work gets done.

"She can handle it. She's a
solider." – my dad tells my
dentist with pride when he
questions taking out all of my 4
wisdom teeth in one shot.

It's harder for me to work at a
70% level rather than at my
usual 120%.

Less than 4 hours of sleep is
hard – the sleep apnea doesn't
help either.

If I get rattled, I have a talk
with myself and get back on
track immediately. This is how I
operate.

My fat self: part 2

When you see the rolls on your
body reducing but the results
are still not reflected in photos
— I used to be so photogenic
that my even my skinny friends
were jealous. Sigh.

I'm convinced mirrors carry
energy. How else do I look so
good in some and hideous in
others? – it can't be in *my head*.

When you fight with your inner
self to not be mean with the
rolls as you pass by the mirror.

I HATE when women speak
about dieting in the presence of
the male human.

The way I feel about myself doesn't always stay consistent in all situations. I'm still working on this.

My "pearly-whites"

My cousin knows. She knows
that the ONLY insult that will
actually rattle me is about my
teeth.

I carry floss – In. Every. Bag.

"Even when I'm old. Like old
old—I will still have all my
teeth." – I tell my dentist
(again) at my 6-month cleaning.

Teeth. The only physical
attribute that I can't bend on
when it comes to a potential
partner. No. I don't care about
that. Really. Argh.

The look on people's faces
when they realize I don't *want*
anything *in return.*

— *my type of "drug"*

Men's ego

How's it possible for it to be so
easily bruised and inflated so
quickly?

Unfortunately, you don't realize
how easily manipulated you are
by your gender counterpart.

You say you don't want drama
and nagging, but these exact
acts are what validate your
manhood.

Why do my personal and career
accomplishments make you feel
less than?

Me wanting you by my side is
much more significant than
needing you.

Mama bear

This is what I would have done
had I had one:

"Go give grandma and grandpa
a kissie."

We stand when our elders walk
in. Every. Time.

Be kind not only to the other
humans but also to the nature
and animals which surround
you.

Always TRY. Even if you don't
succeed there won't be any
regrets.

You are loved. Unconditionally.

Perspective is everything.
Choose the right side.

There's power in asking for
help.

Never give up. You come from
a powerful empire. Don't forget
who you are.

Don't do anything too stupid.
Regular stupid is OK. Know
the difference. I've taught you
better.

Never be afraid to go against
the grain. Create your own
standards and don't give a shit
about what others say, think or
do.

There really is a silver lining to
every situation—you just have
to have the ability to *see* it.

There isn't a better *fix* than
spending time with your family.
Cherish these moments. They
pass way too quickly.

Technology

Zombies. I look around and all
I see are glued eyes on the little
screens in their hands. How is
this even possible when we are
all in the park together?

Put down the phone and let's
talk. You don't have to "check
in" your location. Be present
with me instead.

"Hey, remember those times
when we would just show up to
the pre-determined destination
without changing the time and
location 50 times?"

I love it when the power goes
out. We are all forced to sit and
have a proper conversation
with one another.

The effects and consequences
will only really reveal
themselves when we've already
fallen over the edge.

Pasta, ice-cream and ghormeh sabzi

It has taken a very long time to
learn and to understand that I
don't have to (and shouldn't)
indulge in my favourite foods:
All. The. Time.

It's no longer a coping
mechanism. Much. Ok —a little
bit still but at least I'm aware of
it now.

Apparently, it's a thing to *not* be
full all the time. Hmm.
Someone should have told my
grandma that.

Serve pasta, sangria and cream
puffs at my funeral: Knowing
how to go out with a bang even
in the afterlife.

"You hungry?" – is that actually
a question?

Stupid exercise

I swear. If it didn't actually
work and make me feel so
good: I would just let heart
disease and diabetes wash over
me like a cool refreshing class
of sangria.

"No. I love it." – I hang up the
phone on my brother when I
ask him if he hates exercising
too.

"What's your favourite winter
activity?" Drinking coffee at a
coffee shop while reading and
people watching. Pasta. What?
Those are activities too!

Apparently, it's another *thing* to
prioritize exercise. Argh.

I hike up to the top back row
of the movie theatre: I thought
I was being funny on my dating
profile. Status: still single.

Grateful

I am grateful for my mom's
love that has nourished us,
guided us and blessed us
throughout our whole life.

Children's laughter is the
closest sound we humans can
hear made by the angels.

The accessibility to clean water
and electricity. Also, no bombs
dropping is really great too!

Blessed to have had the friends
I have in my life.

When things *flow* without any
effort or push.

Human male teenager

"You see this whole section.
You will need one of each" – at
the local drug store pointing at
deodorant, body wash and
body spray.

You're a stinky teenager:
Shower DAILY. When you
think you don't need to shower
that day. Take TWO!

Be kind and conscientious: She
feels things a thousand times
more than you. Remember
what I told you: The human
female is light years ahead of
you: Fact. Just deal with it.

I don't care about what type of work you go into. The only thing that matters is that you're happy doing it. That's really a thing. Believe me.

"You're the kid I never wanted." ¿What? That's a compliment.

Your biological mom understands how much I love you.

You are a rare breed of the human male: You have a golden heart.

You already know that we won't like her. So, try your best to pick a really good one even though your predecessors haven't held up their end of the bargain either. Myself included.

I look forward to hearing glee in your voice and fire in your eyes when you speak about a future aspiration: only witnessed this so far when you talk about your superhero movies.

Shooku aka "Little Penguin" aka Grandma

"Maman, I'm so tired of this
rain. ¿When will it stop?"
"My dear, don't you see the
trees moving and dancing?
Look at how happy they are"
– *Perspective*

"Look at this little lady,
Honey—Look at how
beautifully she's grown." – She
points at her blossoming pots
of flowers surrounding her.

EVERY. Single. Thing she
cooks!

She gave me her wedding ring:
fits perfectly!

"Shookooli. My Penguin. Do
you know how much I love
you?"

"Naneh, *manam hameentoor*" –
her eyes fill with instant tears as
she pulls me in for the hug.
This. THIS is where HOME is.

"I don't want to stay here any longer. Why did you guys not talk me out of this?"

My aunt's response, "There's a reason it's called *experience*!"

– Finished my one-year contract and after what seemed like a lifetime of chasing **one** goal. **I now finally had clarity.**

Wolfy

"Just listen to what he says" my
best friend encourages me to
listen to the preacher on TV.

"I don't like him. What he says
doesn't match his eyes. I can
tell. He really does bad things. I
know you can *see* that".

"Just listen" she repeats,
annoyed.

Then it came—the one line that
finally pushed me to let go of it
all!

"The betrayal wasn't meant to
break you, but rather to make
you stronger."

The wolf on the TV screen
finally said something I
believed.

These standards though…

I don't do things the normal
way. Never have. Jump into the
deep deep end. Hell! I jump
into the tsunami—this is the
standard I have created for
myself.

Note to self: It's ok if we don't
have every fucking thing
figured out and on schedule
ALL the fucking time.

Apparently most other humans
don't behave like this. Glad I'm
not one of *those* people. Whew!

You mean it's not normal to
ask ALL the questions on the
FIRST date?

Just realized I don't have to
give a flying fuck as to which
finger I wear my rings on.
¿How did this just dawn on me
now?

"Fuck you, cultural and societal
norms" – I say while I wave my
left ring finger in the air.

All the powers

I have a staring problem.
Really. I have to actively tell
myself that other's whom I'm
staring at can see me 'cause I'm
not invisible.

I'm really sharp. I pick up on
other people's behavioural
reactions and emotions really
quickly: It can become really
overwhelming at times.

Any superpower? I'd want to
fly. Just have to work on my
debilitating fear of heights. I
told you I wasn't normal.

Why would I ask for help when
I can just do EVERYTHING
myself. All. The. Time.

An ode to coffee

I roll out of bed because I
know I'm minutes away from
consuming you.

Favourite customer service job:
Barista.

The smell is almost as good as a
newborn baby. Almost. Better
than a brand-new car for sure
though. Hands down.

Yes. I guess we are a lot alike:
full of energy and pack a punch
depending on intensity. Yup.
Sounds about right.

Everything that I go through that you don't

There's a human growing inside of her. So, yeah, it's ok if she's swollen, cranky and doesn't want to be nice. A human! Inside her body!!

Every month. EVERY. SINGLE. MONTH. For 40 years. And men complain about fucking allergies and headaches. If you only *knew*.

I can't even adjust my bra without first looking around to make sure no one is looking, and you re-adjust EVERYTHING. In plain public display as though, no one sees you're digging for gold!!

I can't even express being
exhausted from my monthly
visitor without you rolling your
eyes at me as though I'm
making up the absolute
exhaustion I go through.
Asshole, I go through Super+
tampons the first FOUR days!
Can u even fathom the
shedding my body is going
through?!

Chocolate and pasta. I crave
even more when I'm coming
on. And during. And after.
Never mind. This needs to be
on another list.

Calmness

How do you have so little to
say when you've lived so much?
-- when you start to rethink
how much you *like* the calm
guys.

The sound of the moving water
= definition of stabilization to
my wondering, ADHD, "oh
what's that noise or sparkly
thing", mind.

"Floaty. Floaty. Come in so we
can go and have lunch." -- my
brother calling me in from my
slumber on the Cuban ocean
waters.

"The earth has breathed in the
warmth of the spring to come."
-- my mom says to relieve my
worry of the lingering winter.

Conversations with God

Really though. I'm done. Learnt
all the lessons. All of them.
Don't need to come back again!

I know you exist by the
complexity and absolute beauty
visible in nature and animals.
The humans though. A little
less.

I talk to my plants. It's
something I've learnt from my
Little Penguin. I know they can
hear me! ꕥHow else would they
be growing so fast?

ꕥDid you purposely make the
male human so dense and
selfish? Was that just a joke on
us? Glad you're getting a kick
out of it. Sigh.

Also, this period thing. ʕYou mean to tell me there wasn't ANY other way to accomplish the end goal? Really?!

I think about my karmic footprint. All. The time. ---I hope I'm *doing* it right.

Why did you make this love thing so emotional?

Kudos on: Chocolate. Sunsets. The absolute joy and innocence in children's eyes. Warm hugs and hearty laughs that feel like they last forever and which you feel in your stomach. And sex —This one was your best work yet. Kudos. Really.

Most importantly, I know you exist because you gave me my mom. Thank you.

We go to great extents to visit
other countries in hopes of
learning more about their
culture, people and all their
every-thingness.

Yet we treat those in our own
countries who are different and
don't share the same colour,
beliefs or orientations with
condemnation.

— This is where I ask: What
the hell is going on?! Are we all
hypocrites living in sheep's
clothing?!

My little ladies

You are much more powerful
than what the popular media
has allowed for you to believe.

When you wear your short
shorts, unfortunately you are
judged. Yes. In every way!
Don't get mad, I didn't make
the rules.

So many years have to pass by
before you realize that it really
is OK to be different and to be
your real authentic self.

Hear me little ladies:

-- the best thing you can do, is
to embrace every aspect of who
you are and move forward
proud and strong

-- don't give a shit about not
having the "right" anything

-- remember there's beauty in
imperfections

-- know that all other human
females also have their own
insecurities – yes, even the
skinny ones!

-- trust me when I say the size
of your thighs, hips, stomach,
arms or any other part of you
that you might love less is not
indicative of meeting someone
who is worthy of you

*People watching: one of my favourite
pastimes*

-- the little sunshine feeding his
mommy a spoonful of ice
cream while she was kneeling to
meet his glorious offer

-- they are literally just sitting in
front of each other and not
saying anything. ⸮How's that
even possible?

-- when the guy beside me at
my favourite coffee shop *side
glances* me for talking too loud
on my phone with my
Khaleh—dude! we're in a
coffee shop not the freakin'
library!

Vous/Tu/Shoma/Toh

She says shoma when speaking
to me—this in some ways is
harder to adjust to than
"ma'am".

I never thought this transition
to vous/shoma would ever
actually come for me – (mostly
because in my head I look so
young).

"Ma'am, I'm just being
respectful."

The White Coats vs. my size 18 body

Trying to convince the medical professional that even liquid gel medication is super strong for me—Yes even though I'm THIS size—It's because of what I DON'T put into my body!

When you have to defend yourself in the hospital to get the same treatment as an average size body: "No I don't have diabetes! I'm here because of the stomach flu."

I wish they'd see my results first before my size 18 body.

The lens

When you shock people by
your confidence—they weren't
expecting this because I'm a big
girl.

You know how some of us can
look into the mirror and see
our body much bigger than it
really is? --- I've been blessed
with the opposite lens!

People's reactions to the space
I take up that makes me think
they see me with another lens.

I don't get why you admire or
want to look like women who
have the "looks" they do
because of surgery. ؟Am I the
only one that thinks that's
absolute insanity?

My fellow human females:

-- this is how we give up our power. When we believe the popular narrative about having to have surgery to change our bodies because we are constantly told that if we don't fit into the cookie-fucking-cut-mould, we are not good enough!

You are MORE than Enough. In every WAY. Don't listen to them. (They are robbing us of our *every-thingness* that has been bestowed upon us).

To the hot summery day—I
thank you.

I thank you for finally feeling
warmth deep in my bones.

I thank you for the golden sun-
kissed skin you have given me.

I thank you for filling me with
so much energy that I'm able to
complete so many of my To-
Do's in one day.

I even thank you for my sweat
stained shirt and inner thigh
friction burn.

Don't listen to the Pitta bodied
humans; stay here—stay here
for as long as you like—stay
here to fill us of all that winter
has taken away.

Collaboration over competition

When we are able to come
together and to lift one another
up for the greater good—that's
what it is all about.

Your success empowers me.
Not the other way around.

Basking in the glory of success
is even more joyful when there
are others who have also been
able to benefit from the
success.

flow: when the ease of
synchronicity and serendipity
merge to allow for all the
necessary pieces to fit with one
another.

My little ladies: Part 2

You impress me with your
wokeness and integrity that you
display at such a young age.

Know that I stand beside you
as a pillar of support—You are
NEVER alone. Remember that.

Your energy, drive and tenacity
to want to change and question
the system will out rule the nay-
sayers and skeptics. Keep at it.

When in doubt revert to your
truth: your family, friends and
values. Deep down, you will
know the path you have to stay
on.

About the Author

Hanieh Khoshkhou was born in Iran and immigrated to Canada when she was eight years old. Her professional background has revolved around education, curriculum and program development, management, and community development.

It is only because she thinks she is so awesome that she has also dabbled in this writing thing.

In her spare time, Hanieh enjoys basking with the easy notion that if she wanted to, she could become an astronaut.

She values honesty, compassion, and above everything and anything else, she wants to make a difference in this world.

Take it all in.

She is 100% serious about it all.